FIBONACCI
Discovering the Golden Sequence Behind Nature

A Coloring Book for Adults

Illustrated by Marija Mladenović

Copyright © 2017 Parachute Coloring Books

All rights reserved. No part of this publication may be reproduced, distributed, or transmitted in any form or by any means, scanning, photocopying, recording, or other electronic or mechanical methods, without express written permission of the publisher.

Fibonacci Sequence: The Golden Thread Between Math and Nature

There are some things in life that can truly move us and inspire us to do great things. Originally popularized by the Italian mathematician known as Fibonacci, born Leonardo of Pisa (c.1170 – c. 1250), the Fibonacci Sequence has captivated the attention of scientists, artists and architects for centuries.

How does it work? In the sequence, each number is the sum of the two numbers before it:

1, 1, 2, 3, 5, 8, 13, 21, 34, 55, 89, 144, 233, 377, ...

One interesting fact about Fibonacci numbers is that the ratio of each successive pair of numbers in the sequence is very close to the Golden Ratio. The Golden Ratio is a unique ratio, used by Leonardo DaVinci in his paintings, by the Greeks in architecture, and is still used today by many professionals for the same reason: its pleasing aesthetic effects.

The sequence can be interpreted geometrically, where each number is represented by a square:

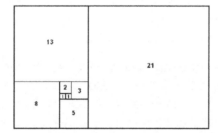

If we draw a spiral starting from the first square, connecting each succeeding square's opposite corners we have the Fibonacci Spiral:

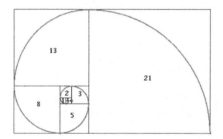

Now, you still might be asking yourself, "What is so special about these numbers?" To answer that question, we have to give nature a closer look. Fibonacci numbers occur in nature to such an extent, that we could say nature operates in a mathematical pattern. Let's see some ways in which we can observe the Fibonacci sequence:

Single spiral: Have you notice how the snail shell has a spiral that looks just like the Fibonacci Spiral? We can also find similar design in seahorse tails, nautilus shells, goat horns and even hurricanes.

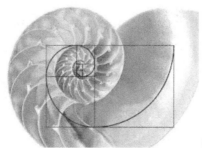

IMAGE 1: Nautilus shell

Numerous spirals: Let's use the sunflower to illustrate this example. Looking closely, you can see spirals curving left and right. When counting these spirals, the total tends to match a Fibonacci number.

IMAGE 2: Spirals in sunflower

Pinecones, pineapples and succulent plants are other examples of multiple spirals. But it's not just for aesthetics, the spiral pattern has a function: for seeds, it enables the plant to pack efficiently the most amount of seeds; and for leaves, it allows best sunlight exposure.

Face and body proportions: On our faces, the ratio between the distances of our mouth to our nose and our eyes to the bottom of our chin, is equal to the Golden Ratio. This isn't just exclusive to the human face, as it can be found in our bodies and on other animals. The Golden Ratio is also found on the beautiful design of the tiger's face, on the butterfly and dragonfly body and wings and the design of the peacock's feather.

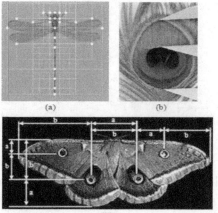

IMAGE 3: Golden Ratio in (a) dragonfly, (b) peacock's feather and (c) butterfly

The beauty of Fibonacci numbers is even present inside all living things, in the DNA molecule: the program for all life. The DNA measures 34 angstroms long by 21 angstroms wide for each full cycle of its double helix spiral. As we know 34 and 21 are successive numbers in the Fibonacci series. Isn't it amazing?

We hope this coloring book can inspire you to look at nature with even more wonder.

Now, to the fun part: Coloring!

Sources and images: http://io9.gizmodo.com/5985588/15-uncanny-examples-of-the-golden-ratio-in-nature;
http://article.sapub.org/10.5923.j.arts.20110101.01.html; https://en.wikipedia.org/wiki/Fibonacci_number
http://www.christianitytoday.com/behemoth/2016/issue-50-june-9-2016/eagle-shell-and-sunflower.html

COLOR TEST PAGE

COLOR TEST PAGE

The Colors of Fall
Coloring Book

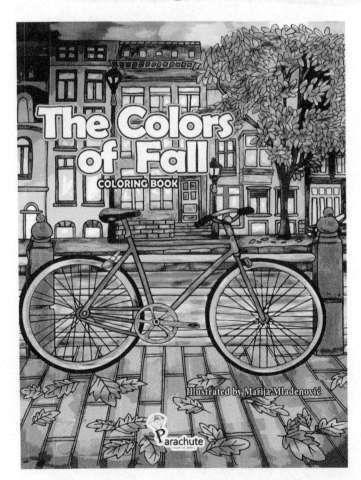

Mother & Daughter
A Narrative Coloring Book

AVAILABLE OCTOBER
Mother & Son
A Narrative Coloring Book

AVAILABLE OCTOBER
Swimwear Evolution

Dear Coloring Book Enthusiast,

Thank you for purchasing our book. We hope you enjoyed coloring it!
If you have any suggestions or complaints, please reach out to us on our Facebook page. We are a small independent business and we strive to make our customers happy. Your opinion matters to us!

Also, make sure you follow us for free coloring pages, and a sneak peek of our latest books at:

 @parachutecoloringbooks

/parachutecoloringbooks

And if you loved this coloring book:
- LEAVE US A REVIEW ON AMAZON -
This way you will help us to reach other coloring enthusiasts like you!

Made in the USA
Las Vegas, NV
04 April 2024